About the Author

Dr. Kamal got his Ph.D. degree in philosophy from Duquesne University, Pittsburgh PA, in 2013. A scholar in residence at Simon Silverman Phenomenology Center-Duquesne University. In addition to a publication of a collection of poems in 2007 and another collection of poems in 2021, he published a philosophical book in 2008 available in the libraries of New York University, University of Pennsylvania, and Alexandria Library. He published another philosophical book in 2023.

Thus Says the Bird

Kamal Shlbei

Thus Says the Bird

Olympia Publishers
London

www.olympiapublishers.com
OLYMPIA PAPERBACK EDITION

Copyright © Kamal Shlbei 2023

The right of Kamal Shlbei to be identified as author of
this work has been asserted in accordance with sections 77 and 78 of
the Copyright, Designs and Patents Act 1988.

All Rights Reserved

No reproduction, copy or transmission of this publication
may be made without written permission.
No paragraph of this publication may be reproduced,
copied or transmitted save with the written permission of the publisher,
or in accordance with the provisions
of the Copyright Act 1956 (as amended).

Any person who commits any unauthorized act in relation to
this publication may be liable to criminal
prosecution and civil claims for damage.

A CIP catalogue record for this title is
available from the British Library.

ISBN: 978-1-80439-049-8

This is a work of fiction.
Names, characters, places and incidents originate from the writer's
imagination. Any resemblance to actual persons, living or dead, is
purely coincidental.

First Published in 2023

Olympia Publishers
Tallis House
2 Tallis Street
London
EC4Y 0AB

Printed in Great Britain

Be Light as a Feather

(1)

As long as the rain does not begin, I am on my balcony
Later
I stand behind the windows
Watching the rain
Falling
drop
by
drop.

(2)

I see drops moving to a river
I see a river flowing into a sea
I see a sea calm as a blue paper
I write notes on the face of the sea.

(3)

And the bird says,
What you write is what you read
What you read is what you write
Mix them
And fly
Far away
Far away.

(4)

You were behind the shade of necessity
You were a nomad in the land of possibility

Link this with that
And be
The necessity of the possibility
The possibility of the necessity.

(5)

Between your voice and me is a space of silence
Let me go.

(6)

And the bird says,
Wherever you go, you meet with a bird
Each bird is an emotion
Each emotion moves in space of probability.

(7)

I am not compatible with emotions moving in space of probability!

(8)

You are probably a bird
You are probably a space
You are a bird flying in a space of probability.

(9)

How can I become a bird flying in a space of probability?
How can I extend myself to reach you?

(10)

That is you,
Says the bird.
Standing in the middle of nothing
Nothing prevents you from you
Nothing except you.

***

(11)

Here I am however
Siting with myself
Feeling much tired!

(12)

And the bird says,
This is not your habit to feel tired when you sit with yourself
How come you become tired?

(13)

I do not know
I just know my way to a rose.

(14)

Let us then begin from the moment when the wind reverses its direction

From the moment when the river changes its way.

(15)

I lost the compass in the sand while I was drinking a cup of water
The sun was bright
The air was fresh
And I was sleepy
Like a tired child,
dreaming of fields of orange
Like a wild horse,
running in vast plateaus
Like a flock of birds,
Heading to the sky.

(16)

And the bird says,
Forget your name for a moment
Return to me
Listen
Between what you see and what you hear is a point of melting
Fix your eyes on it
And fly
Far away
Far away.

(17)

Listen

Do not tell the almond tree about your journey
Keep silent when the shady side of the heart beats and beats
Ascend if you can
to a level of rain
And fall
drop
by
drop.

(18)

I do not see except drops moving toward a river
A river touching the face of the sea.

(19)

Look
There is still a drop of water in the cup
Reflect your face upon it
And see.

(20)

What you see is what has been
And what has been is what you see
Go within what you see
To be
A small bird forgetting its way to the nest
A group of birds knowing their way to the sky.

(21)

Let open for you a window to the sky
You can see a rainbow and some birds
You can see me.

***

(22)

I woke up early that day
I prepared my breakfast with a dream of morning
I was looking for something
I forget the difference between here and there
I confused the bird with a leaf of a tree flying in the wind.

(23)

And the bird says,
Wherever you fly, you find a sky of visions
Wherever the sky is, there you are.

(24)

What should I do in a sky full of visions?
How can I distinguish between a vision and a vision?
Who can save me from a sky of visions?
Let me go.

(25)

Do not go,

Says the bird.
Sit beside the nearest tree
Relax
Open your heart
Let the air enter
Stay for a while
Be silent
And when you hear a voice of a bird
Raise up
Raise up.

(26)

Push me further
Further and further
Let me count the motion of the lights
And when no light approaches the vision of a seeing
Let me see.

(27)

I see you, a vision of tales.
See me, a tale of visions.

***

(28)
White roses on top of a hill
Children playing near a tree
A group of birds flying over and over
A blue sky

A young girl[1] walking with her uncle
What a wonderful afternoon!

(29)

And the bird says,
I was there
You did not see me
I was there
Touching the air while you were looking for something.

(30)

Did you find something?
Anything
A voice of a bird for instance
Anything.

(31)

I am still searching for a bird flying with winds
I am still between wind and wind.

(32)

And the bird says,
Beyond what you think is a logic of a bird
Beyond what you feel is a bird of a logic.

Rawan the daughter of Marwan, the brother of the poet. [1]

(33)

Now listen again
Do you know that your fingers are birds of feelings?
And between a feeling and a feeling is a feeling?
You are now a combination of feelings
Each feeling is a bird
Each bird is you.

(34)

Be light as a feather
Do not ask where you are flying
Lit your vision
Fly.

***

(35)

As soon as I return to my balcony
As soon as I open the windows
I see a bird
waving at me.

(36)

And the bird says,
It looks like you are drawing ships on the sea
How many ships are moving toward the sun?

(37)

As possible as it could be
As many as it could be.

(38)

And the bird sighs,
Nice that you wash the reason by the water of the heart
Nice that you know the distance between a cup of coffee and a book
Nice that you are here
Nice that you are there.

You Will See

(1)

Let us see
Flowers are flourishing
Birds are flying over a sea.

(2)

Let us measure the distance between
A flower and a flower
A bird and a bird
A sea and a sea.

(3)

Let us confuse one flower with another flower
One bird with another bird
One sea with another sea.

(4)

Let us consider a sea as a book of birds
Each bird is a wave
Each wave is a vision
Each vision leads to a sea.

(5)

Let us recount our memories
We select some dreams
We put them one beside the other

And when the picture is not complete
When no dream is the dream
We see what we see
Birds
Areas of emotions
Dreams emerging in light
We see what we see.

(6)

Let us return to a point in the sky
We imagine ourselves as lines extending in a space
As numbers distributed in a differential way
As figures distributed in an artificial way
Here
And
There.

(7)

I cannot figure you out
I cannot even distinguish you from the rest of the figures
Can you be more figural?

(8)

Let us then open for you another way
You are walking now
When you reach the other side of the sea
Sit
You will see.

(9)

You are now free as never before
Ascend further
No matter how disturbing the distance is
Ascend further
Be patient
When you reach upward
Look upward
And
See.

(10)

When you see the lights
Under the shadows of the trees
Enlighten in the light of the lights.

(11)

You will see.

(12)

Extend further in your naked vision
Swim
And
Swim.

(13)

To the last wave
To the last breath
To the last moment
To the degree it becomes impossible.

(14)

You will see.

(15)

How can I become a smooth dream broken on a naked vision?

(16)

How can I follow the steps of rain until I become a garden for forgettable flowers?

(17)

As if you are a cloud searching for a rain
As if you are raining
Now
On the fields
Raining
Now.

(18)

Excited by the raining of me
In the confusion of directions
I direct myself

And
See.

(19)

Let me summarize what I see
I see rain
Content of a possibility
A reality that it is
An unknown bird in itself.

Sit Beside Me

(1)

Come in with colors of evenings
Sit with pleasures of faces
Push the moon toward my shoulder
Sit beside me.

(2)

This is what I see
Different kinds of skies
Each sky is me.

(3)

This is what I have to do
Open many gardens in the heart
Open many windows onto the sea.

(4)

This is what they should ask when they find me near a river
How many dreams are in your bucket?
Did you touch the sun while it is setting down?
Did you talk to the moon while it is shining up?

(5)

This is how a cup of coffee is a reflection of a moment
Just a reflection

This is how a table is a summary of a day
Just a summary.

(6)

This is a tiny speech
Just a tiny speech
Forget about the details
Just a tiny speech
As if you ask someone about the history of the distant woods
As if you wonder about the climate
Could it be rain tomorrow?
Could it be snow?

(7)

This is how I speak when the rain comes
The rain is an angel
The angel is a letter
The letter opens itself to the many
The many are one
The one is many.

(8)

This is how a dew point looks when it is shining
So beautiful!

(9)

This is how the orchestra draws its tune
Sometimes here
Sometimes there.

(10)

This is how the river follows its way
Deeply
Deeply.

(11)

This is how a bird of morning sings
Good morning to all of you.

(12)

This is how the storm looks when it is on the horizon
So frightening!

(13)

This is how a book becomes a Facebook
Today, we are here
Tomorrow, we are there.

(14)

This is how the streets look when no one is there
Looks empty
Looks cold.

(15)

This is how I repeat my name in front of you
I imagine myself a sparrow flying over a thousand moons
And when you call for me
Near your face
Exactly
Near the side of your smile
When you are smiling
I smell you
A collection of beautiful things.

(16)

This is what I mean when I am puzzled
No meaning is the meaning
Close your book
Open your window.

(17)

This is half of the truth
The other half is stolen in the market.

(18)

This is what you could do when you feel anxious
Rest your head on the cheek of the moon
And
Take a nap!

(19)

This is how I see the morning
So bright!

(20)

This is how I see the evening
So glorious!

(21)

This is where I found a stone of hope near a river of anxiety
I was picturing life with a light
I was reflecting on me.

(22)

This is what I see when I stand in the presence of me
Ways of being.

(23)

This is between you and me.

(24)

This is less than a tiny story
Forget about the details.

(25)
Now I tell you,

This is how I reflect you when I look in the mirror
I stretch the distance so it captures the remains of something
That something is a picture of colors
Two colorful pictures are parallelly run
One is you
The other is me.

I Am a Being

(1)

I am a being
A dew point on the face of the morning
When the sun arises
I evaporate into my being
I become a pencil in the hand of the moon
I write notes
I open windows
I smile
I think
I dream.

(2)

I am a being
A mooring star
When the sun arises
I disappear
When the sun sets
I appear.

(3)

I am a being
Just a cup of tea.

(4)

Later
When the café is empty

When the visitors are leaving
When the place is empty
When I have to leave
Something happens
As if the train arrives late
As if I should leave the café early
Later
When I am just a cup of tea
I sit alone
In the empty café
Open the book
And
Read.

(5)

I am a being
A moment in the history of the beings
Sometimes near a garden full of flowers
Sometimes near a river running to its being
I sit
Alone
Looking at the horizon of the beings
I wonder
How beautiful it is!